contents

NZ, Canada, US and UK readers

Please note that Australian cup and spoon
measurements are metric. A quick conversion
chart appears on page 63.

tips to a sure-fire success

Char-grills and barbecues are, traditionally, a relaxed affair. Easy food cooked in a convivial atmosphere is the aim; follow these commonsense tips to ensure that your next gathering is a resounding success.

The verbs "grill" and "barbecue" are often used interchangeably; they refer to cooking food on a grill, grill plate or flat hot plate over a heat source, such as electricity, gas, or a charcoal or wood fire. There are many different styles and sizes of grill plates and pans, made from a variety of materials ranging from cast iron to aluminium and those with a non-stick surface; all are suitable for stove-top grilling. Read on for char-grilling and barbecuing tips…

- Organisation is the key to success... first and foremost, if you plan to cook on an outdoor fuelled barbecue, check there's enough gas in the gas bottle, or that you have sufficient wood or charcoal. Next, place all utensils, sauces, etc., within arm's reach before you begin.
- Start with a clean grill or barbecue plate, i.e., one that's free from burned-on food from previous usage.
- Thoroughly heat the barbecue or grill plate before starting to cook.
- Keep the grill pan or plate lightly oiled to prevent food from sticking to it.
- If you are cooking kebabs, prepare the skewers ahead of time. Soak bamboo skewers in water for at least an hour before threading meat/vegetables onto them, to prevent them from scorching during cooking. If using metal skewers, lightly oil them before threading meat/vegetables onto them, to prevent the food from sticking to the skewers.
- Don't salt meat before cooking, as it draws out the juices. If salt is necessary, add it just before the end of cooking time.
- Bring food to room temperature before you start cooking.
- Never use an aerosol can of cooking-oil spray on a barbecue that is alight, or over a gas flame.
- When using aluminium foil, always wrap the food with the shiny side facing inwards, towards the food.
- Always use glass or ceramic dishes for marinating food; metal can taint flavours.
- To avoid burning food that has been marinated in a mix containing sugar or honey, cook food over medium rather than high heat.
- It is best to sear meat on each side over high heat for a few minutes, then move it to a cooler part of the grill plate to continue cooking as desired. Turn meat once only to retain juices and flavour, and to avoid toughening.
- Use tongs or a slide to turn meat (a fork pierces the meat, causing loss of juices). Never cut meat to see if it is cooked; instead, press the meat with tongs – rare feels soft, medium will offer a little resistance and well-done will feel firm when pressed.

scotch fillet steaks with caramelised onion and garlic mushrooms

6 beef scotch fillet
steaks (1.25kg)
1/2 cup (125ml) dry
red wine
2 tablespoons chopped
fresh basil leaves
2 cloves garlic, crushed
20g butter
6 medium red onions
(1kg), sliced thinly
1/3 cup (75g) firmly
packed brown sugar
1/4 cup (60ml)
red wine vinegar
6 large flat
mushrooms (840g)
2 tablespoons olive oil
1 clove garlic,
crushed, extra
1 teaspoon
lemon pepper

Combine beef, wine, basil and garlic in large
bowl. Cover; refrigerate 3 hours or overnight.
Melt butter in large frying pan; cook onion,
stirring, until soft and browned lightly. Stir in
sugar and vinegar; cook, stirring constantly,
about 20 minutes or until onion is well browned
and mixture thickened.
Brush mushrooms with combined oil, extra garlic
and lemon pepper; cook on heated oiled grill plate
or barbecue until tender.
Drain beef; discard marinade. Cook beef,
in batches, on heated oiled grill plate or barbecue
until browned and cooked as desired.
Top each piece of beef with a mushroom and
a little caramelised onion.

serves 6
per serving 21.9g fat; 2069kJ (495 cal)

salt and pepper chicken skewers on baby bok choy

8 chicken thigh fillets (880g), chopped coarsely
1 teaspoon sichuan peppercorns, crushed
$^1/_2$ teaspoon five-spice powder
2 teaspoons sea salt
1 teaspoon sesame oil
600g baby bok choy, quartered
1 tablespoon oyster sauce
1 teaspoon soy sauce
1 tablespoon chopped fresh coriander

Thread chicken onto 12 skewers. Combine peppercorns, five-spice and salt in small bowl; sprinkle mixture over chicken, then press in firmly.
Cook chicken, in batches, on heated oiled grill plate or barbecue until browned and cooked through.
Meanwhile, heat oil in wok or large frying pan; stir-fry bok choy with combined sauces until just wilted.
Divide bok choy among serving plates; top with chicken skewers. Serve sprinkled with coriander.

serves 4
per serving 17.4g fat; 1417kJ (339 cal)
tip You need 12 skewers for this recipe; if using bamboo skewers, soak them in water for an hour before use to prevent them from splintering or scorching.

cajun cutlets with cucumber salsa

12 lamb cutlets (900g)
2 teaspoons ground cumin
2 teaspoons ground coriander
1 teaspoon ground turmeric
1 teaspoon sweet paprika
1 teaspoon ground oregano
1 teaspoon chilli powder
$\frac{1}{2}$ teaspoon ground clove
2 tablespoons olive oil
cucumber salsa
2 lebanese cucumbers (260g), seeded, chopped
2 medium tomatoes (260g), seeded, chopped
1 medium yellow capsicum (200g), chopped
2 green onions, chopped finely
1 tablespoon balsamic vinegar
1 tablespoon olive oil

Coat lamb with combined spices and oil in large bowl. Cover, refrigerate 3 hours or overnight.
Cook lamb, in batches, on heated oiled grill plate or barbecue until browned and cooked as desired. Serve lamb with cucumber salsa.
Cucumber salsa Combine ingredients in small bowl, cover; refrigerate 30 minutes.

serves 4
per serving 28.4g fat; 1994kJ (477 cal)

five-spice chicken

750g chicken tenderloins
1 teaspoon peanut oil
1$\frac{1}{2}$ teaspoons five-spice powder
2 cloves garlic, crushed
250g hokkien noodles
300g baby corn
500g asparagus
1 medium red capsicum (200g), sliced thinly
$\frac{1}{4}$ cup chopped fresh flat-leaf parsley

Combine chicken, oil, five-spice and garlic
in medium bowl.
Cook chicken, in batches, on heated oiled
grill plate or barbecue until browned and
cooked through.
Meanwhile, place noodles in medium
heatproof bowl; cover with boiling water,
separate with fork, drain.
Cut baby corn in half. Snap woody ends
off asparagus; chop remaining spears into
same-sized pieces as halved corn. Stir-fry corn,
asparagus and capsicum in heated lightly oiled wok
or large frying pan until just tender; add noodles.
Stir parsley into vegetables off the heat,
then divide mixture among serving dishes;
top with chicken.

serves 4
per serving 16.1g fat; 1647kJ (394 cal)

lamb with chermoulla

2 tablespoons grated lemon rind
2 cloves garlic, chopped coarsely
2 small fresh red chillies, seeded, chopped coarsely
1 tablespoon grated fresh ginger
1/4 cup chopped fresh flat-leaf parsley
1/4 cup chopped fresh coriander
1 teaspoon sweet paprika
1/4 cup (60ml) olive oil
8 lamb forequarter chops (1.5kg)

Blend or process rind, garlic, chilli, ginger, herbs, paprika and oil until well combined. Place lamb in single layer in shallow dish; coat lamb in chermoulla paste. Cover; refrigerate 3 hours or overnight.
Cook lamb, in batches, on heated oiled grill plate or barbecue until browned and cooked as desired. Serve with a mixed salad and lemon wedges, if desired.

serves 4
per serving 30.4g fat; 2103kJ (503 cal)

chicken tenderloins in green peppercorn and tarragon dressing

2 tablespoons water
2 teaspoons drained green
    peppercorns, crushed
2 teaspoons
    wholegrain mustard
2 green onions, sliced thinly
1 tablespoon chopped
    fresh tarragon
1 tablespoon olive oil
1 tablespoon sugar
1/3 cup (80ml) white
    wine vinegar
4 medium potatoes (800g)
8 chicken tenderloins (600g)
1 tablespoon cracked
    black pepper
4 large tomatoes (1kg),
    sliced thinly
1 medium red onion (170g),
    sliced thinly

Combine the water, peppercorns, mustard, green onion, tarragon, oil, sugar and vinegar in small bowl. Whisk to combine dressing; reserve.

Boil, steam or microwave potato until just tender; drain.

Meanwhile, coat chicken all over in pepper; cook chicken, in batches, on heated oiled grill plate or barbecue until browned and cooked through. Stand 5 minutes; slice thickly.

When potatoes are cool enough to handle, slice thickly. Cook potatoes, in batches, on same heated oiled grill plate or barbecue until browned both sides.

Arrange chicken, potato, tomato and onion slices on serving plates; drizzle with reserved dressing.

serves 4
per serving 13.4g fat; 1789kJ (428 cal)

hoisin pork skewers

750g pork fillet, sliced
1/2 cup (125ml) hoisin sauce
2 tablespoons plum sauce
2 cloves garlic, crushed

Combine pork, sauces and garlic in medium bowl.
Cover, refrigerate 3 hours or overnight.
Thread pork onto 12 skewers. Cook skewers,
in batches, on heated oiled grill plate or barbecue
until browned and cooked through.

serves 4
per serving 6.3g fat; 1250kJ (299 cal)
tip You need 12 skewers for this recipe;
if using bamboo skewers, soak them in water
for an hour before use to prevent them from
splintering or scorching.

thai chicken and rice

2 cups (300g) long-grain white rice
1 cup firmly packed fresh mint leaves
1/3 cup (80ml) sweet chilli sauce
1 tablespoon fish sauce
1 tablespoon soy sauce
1/2 cup (125ml) lime juice
2 teaspoons grated fresh ginger
1/4 cup chopped fresh lemon grass
4 chicken breast fillets (680g)
1 small red capsicum (150g), chopped finely

Cook rice in large saucepan of boiling water,
uncovered, until just tender; drain.
Reserve six mint leaves; blend or process
remaining mint with sauces, juice, ginger and
lemon grass until well combined.
Cook chicken, in batches, on heated oiled grill plate
or barbecue until browned and cooked through.
Toss capsicum through cooked rice, divide
among serving dishes; top with chicken.
Drizzle with sauce; sprinkle with reserved
coarsely chopped mint.

serves 4
per serving 10.6g fat; 2274kJ (544 cal)

seafood salad with gremolata dressing

1kg large uncooked
    prawns
500g squid hoods
500g cleaned baby
    octopus
1/3 cup (80ml) olive oil
2 tablespoons finely
    chopped fresh
    lemon rind
2 cloves garlic,
    chopped finely
1 lebanese
    cucumber (130g)
100g mesclun
2 tablespoons
    lemon juice
2 tablespoons chopped
    fresh flat-leaf parsley

Shell and devein prawns, leaving tails intact.
Cut squid in half lengthways; score inside surface
of each piece, cut into 5cm-wide strips. Remove
and discard heads from octopus.

Combine seafood in large bowl with 1 tablespoon
of the oil, 1 teaspoon of the rind and half of the
garlic, cover; refrigerate 3 hours or overnight.

Cook seafood, in batches, on heated oiled grill plate
or barbecue until prawns are just changed in colour
and squid and octopus are just cooked through.

Using vegetable peeler, slice cucumber into ribbons.
Combine cucumber with mesclun in medium bowl.

Combine juice and parsley with remaining oil,
rind and garlic in screw-top jar; shake well.

Serve seafood on cucumber-mesclun mixture;
drizzle with dressing.

serves 6
per serving 14.7g fat; 1237kJ (296 cal)

lemon basil chicken on hot potato salad

4 chicken thigh
    cutlets (640g)
2 cloves garlic, crushed
2 tablespoons
    lemon juice
1 teaspoon cracked
    black pepper
$1/2$ cup chopped
    fresh basil
5 slices pancetta (75g)
500g tiny new
    potatoes, halved
$1/4$ cup (60g) sour cream
$1/4$ cup (75g) mayonnaise
2 tablespoons drained
    green peppercorns,
    chopped coarsely
2 tablespoons
    french dressing

Combine chicken, garlic, juice, pepper and half of the basil in medium bowl; toss to coat chicken all over in marinade.

Cook chicken, in batches, on heated oiled grill plate or barbecue, brushing occasionally with marinade until browned and cooked through. Cover to keep warm.

Cook pancetta on heated oiled grill plate or barbecue about 1 minute each side or until crisp; chop coarsely.

Meanwhile, boil, steam or microwave potato until just tender; drain. Divide potato among serving plates; drizzle with combined sour cream, mayonnaise, peppercorns, dressing, remaining basil and pancetta. Serve chicken with hot potato salad.

serves 4
per serving 25.2g fat; 1822kJ (436 cal)

vegetable salad

1 large red onion (300g)
8 medium egg tomatoes (600g)
8 baby eggplant (480g)
4 medium zucchini (480g)
4 medium yellow patty-pan squash (120g), halved
2 medium red capsicums (400g), sliced thickly
dressing
1/4 cup (60ml) extra virgin olive oil
1/4 cup (60ml) balsamic vinegar
1 clove garlic, crushed

Cut onion and tomatoes into eight wedges each;
thinly slice eggplant and zucchini lengthways.
Cook onion, tomato, eggplant, zucchini,
squash and capsicum, in batches, on heated
oiled grill plate or barbecue until vegetables are
browned and just tender.
Combine vegetables in large bowl or on
serving platter. Drizzle with dressing; toss
gently to combine.
Dressing Combine ingredients in screw-top
jar; shake well.

serves 8
per serving 7.4g fat; 485kJ (116 cal)

paprika chicken with raisin and coriander pilaf

8 skinless chicken thigh cutlets (1.3kg)
2 tablespoons lemon juice
3 cloves garlic, crushed
1/2 teaspoon hot paprika
1 teaspoon sweet paprika
1 teaspoon ground cinnamon
3/4 cup (200g) yogurt
1 tablespoon olive oil
1 medium brown onion (150g), chopped finely
2 cups (200g) basmati rice
1 litre (4 cups) chicken stock
1/2 cup (85g) chopped raisins
3/4 cup chopped fresh coriander

Combine chicken, juice, garlic and spices in large bowl, cover; refrigerate 3 hours or overnight.
Cook chicken, in batches, on heated oiled grill plate or barbecue, brushing with a little of the yogurt, until browned and cooked through.
Meanwhile, heat oil in medium saucepan; cook onion, stirring, until softened. Add rice; stir to coat in onion mixture. Add stock; bring to a boil. Reduce heat; simmer, covered, stirring occasionally, about 25 minutes or until rice is almost tender. Stir in raisins; cook, covered, 5 minutes.
Stir coriander into pilaf off the heat just before serving. Top pilaf with chicken and remaining yogurt.

serves 4
per serving 11g fat; 2629kJ (629 cal)

mushrooms with herb butter

80g butter, melted
1 teaspoon grated lime rind
1 tablespoon lime juice
1 tablespoon chopped fresh flat-leaf parsley
1 tablespoon chopped fresh basil leaves
6 large flat mushrooms (840g)

Combine butter, rind, juice and herbs in small bowl.
Cook mushrooms on heated oiled grill plate or
barbecue, brushing with half of the butter mixture,
until mushrooms are just tender and well browned.
Serve with remaining butter.

serves 6
per serving 11.1g fat; 477kJ (114 cal)

beef fillet with horseradish mash

4 medium potatoes (800g), chopped coarsely
½ cup (120g) sour cream
¼ cup (60ml) milk
1 tablespoon horseradish cream
600g beef eye fillet
1 cup (250ml) dry red wine
½ cup (125ml) beef stock
1 tablespoon wholegrain mustard

Boil, steam or microwave potato until tender;
drain. Mash potato with sour cream and milk in
large bowl until smooth; stir in horseradish cream.
Meanwhile, slice beef into four equal pieces.
Cook on heated oiled grill plate or barbecue until
browned and cooked as desired. Cover beef,
stand 5 minutes.
Meanwhile, combine wine, stock and mustard in
medium saucepan; bring to a boil. Reduce heat;
simmer, uncovered, until sauce reduces by half.
Serve beef topped with sauce, accompanied
by mash and, if desired, steamed asparagus.

serves 4
per serving 20.7g fat; 2040kJ (488 cal)

asparagus with balsamic dressing

400g asparagus, trimmed
1/3 cup (80ml) extra virgin olive oil
1 1/2 tablespoons balsamic vinegar
2 medium tomatoes (380g), peeled,
    seeded, chopped finely
2 tablespoons small basil leaves

Cook asparagus on heated oiled grill plate
or barbecue until browned and tender.
Serve asparagus drizzled with combined oil,
vinegar and tomato; sprinkle with basil.

serves 4
per serving 18.4g fat; 782kJ (187 cal)

rib-eye steak with vegetables

2 medium red capsicums (400g)
2 small eggplants (460g)
2 medium yellow zucchini (240g)
6 beef scotch fillet steaks (1.25kg)
1 cup (260g) olive paste
1 tablespoon olive oil

Quarter capsicums, remove seeds and membranes. Roast under grill or in very hot oven, skin-side up, until skin blisters and blackens. Cover capsicum pieces with plastic or paper for 5 minutes, peel away skin. Cut eggplant into 2cm slices. Cut zucchini, lengthways, into 2cm slices.

Cook beef, in batches, on heated oiled grill plate or barbecue until browned and cooked as desired; cover to keep warm. Cook capsicum, eggplant and zucchini, in batches, on same grill plate or barbecue, until browned all over and soft.

Top beef with eggplant, zucchini and capsicum. Serve with olive paste; drizzle with olive oil.

serves 6
per serving 17.9g fat; 1676kJ (401 cal)

chilli, tofu and vegetable kebabs

The chillies we used are fiery hot – warn your guests before they eat them!

25 small fresh
   red thai chillies
²/₃ cup (160ml) olive oil
2 teaspoons grated
   lemon rind
¹/₃ cup (80ml) lemon juice
1 tablespoon chopped
   fresh oregano
1 tablespoon chopped
   fresh dill
2 cloves garlic, crushed
300g packet firm
   tofu, drained
1 large red onion (300g)
2 medium zucchini (250g)
6 medium yellow patty-
   pan squash (180g)
12 large cherry
   tomatoes (250g)

Remove and discard seeds from one of the chillies and chop finely.

Combine oil, rind, juice, herbs, garlic and chopped chilli in screw-top jar; shake well.

Cut tofu into 12 even pieces, cut onion into 12 wedges, cut zucchini into 12 pieces and cut each squash in half.

Thread a chilli then a piece of zucchini, tofu, tomato, onion, squash and another chilli onto a skewer. Repeat with remaining skewers, chilli, tofu and vegetables.

Cook kebabs, in batches, on heated oiled grill plate or barbecue, brushing with half of the oil mixture, until vegetables are browned on both sides and just tender, turning only once as the tofu is delicate and breaks easily.

Serve kebabs with the remaining oil mixture.

serves 4
per serving 42g fat; 1927kJ (461 cal)
tip You need 12 skewers for this recipe; if using bamboo skewers, soak them in water for an hour before use to prevent them from splintering or scorching.

veal T-bones with chickpea and tomato salad

4 veal T-bone steaks (750g)
1 teaspoon ground coriander
1 teaspoon ground cumin
1/4 teaspoon chilli powder
2 teaspoons grated lemon rind
1 tablespoon olive oil
chickpea and tomato salad
300g can chickpeas, drained
2 large tomatoes (500g), seeded, chopped
1 small red onion (100g), chopped
2 green onions, chopped finely
2 tablespoons chopped fresh coriander
1 tablespoon chopped fresh mint
1 teaspoon grated lemon rind
1/4 cup (60ml) lemon juice
1/3 cup (80ml) olive oil

Combine veal, spices, chilli, rind and oil in large bowl; cover, refrigerate 3 hours or overnight.
Cook veal, in batches, on heated oiled grill plate or barbecue until browned and cooked as desired.
Serve veal with chickpea and tomato salad.
Chickpea and tomato salad Combine ingredients in medium bowl.

serves 4
per serving 28.9g fat; 1956kJ (468 cal)

lime-marinated lamb loin with herbed couscous

800g lamb eye of loin
2 cloves garlic, sliced thinly
1/4 cup (60ml) lime juice
2 tablespoons olive oil
2 cups (500ml) chicken stock
2 cups (400g) couscous
1/4 cup chopped fresh coriander
yogurt sauce
3/4 cup (200g) yogurt
1/4 cup chopped fresh mint
2 tablespoons lime juice

Combine lamb, garlic, juice and half of the oil in large bowl. Cover; refrigerate 15 minutes.
Meanwhile, place stock and remaining oil in medium saucepan; bring to a boil. Remove from heat; add couscous. Cover; stand about 5 minutes or until liquid is absorbed, fluffing couscous with fork occasionally. Toss coriander through couscous.
Cook lamb, in batches, on heated oiled grill plate or barbecue until browned and cooked as desired.
Stand lamb 5 minutes, then slice thinly and serve with couscous and yogurt sauce.
Yogurt sauce Combine ingredients in small bowl.

serves 4
per serving 19.2g fat; 3081kJ (737 cal)

teriyaki pork with wasabi dressing

750g pork fillets
1/4 cup (60ml) teriyaki marinade
50g snow pea sprouts
100g mesclun
50g watercress, trimmed
1 medium red capsicum (200g), sliced thinly
250g yellow teardrop tomatoes, halved
wasabi dressing
1 1/2 teaspoons wasabi powder
1/4 cup (60ml) cider vinegar
1/3 cup (80ml) vegetable oil
1 tablespoon light soy sauce

Brush pork with teriyaki marinade. Cook pork,
in batches, on heated oiled grill plate or barbecue,
brushing frequently with marinade, until browned
and cooked through; cover to keep warm.
Meanwhile, combine sprouts, mesclun,
watercress, capsicum and tomato in large bowl.
Pour wasabi dressing over salad mixture; toss gently
to combine. Slice pork; serve with salad.
Wasabi dressing Blend wasabi powder with
vinegar in small jug; whisk in remaining ingredients.

serves 4
per serving 23g fat; 1797kJ (430 cal)

sausages with tomato relish

1 tablespoon olive oil
1 clove garlic, crushed
1 medium brown onion (150g), chopped
2 large tomatoes (500g), chopped coarsely
1 tablespoon balsamic vinegar
1 teaspoon brown sugar
1 tablespoon torn fresh basil leaves
8 thin pork sausages

Heat oil in small saucepan, add garlic and onion;
cook, stirring, until browned lightly. Add tomato,
vinegar and sugar; simmer, uncovered, stirring
occasionally, about 20 minutes or until mixture is
reduced by half. Just before serving, add basil.
Meanwhile, cook sausages on heated oiled
grill plate or barbecue until browned and cooked
through. Serve sausages with warm tomato relish.
Sprinkle with extra basil leaves, if desired.

serves 4
per serving 30.5g fat; 1538kJ (368 cal)

greek octopus salad

1/3 cup (80ml) lemon juice
1 tablespoon honey
4 cloves garlic, crushed
1/4 teaspoon cayenne pepper
1kg cleaned baby octopus, halved
100g baby spinach leaves
1 small red onion (100g), sliced thinly
250g cherry tomatoes, halved
1 tablespoon shredded fresh mint
1 tablespoon shredded fresh basil
100g fetta cheese, chopped coarsely

Combine juice, honey, garlic, pepper and octopus in large bowl, cover; refrigerate 3 hours or overnight.
Drain octopus over large bowl; reserve marinade. Cook octopus, in batches, on heated oiled grill plate or barbecue until tender.
Meanwhile, place reserved marinade in small saucepan; bring to a boil. Reduce heat; simmer, uncovered, about 5 minutes or until marinade reduces slightly, cool.
Just before serving, place octopus and marinade in large bowl with remaining ingredients; toss gently to combine.

serves 4
per serving 8.6g fat; 1279kJ (306 cal)
tip You could substitute rocket or any other salad green for the spinach.

prawns with garlic and caper butter

24 large uncooked prawns (1kg)
80g butter
4 cloves garlic, crushed
1 tablespoon drained baby capers, chopped coarsely
1 tablespoon chopped fresh oregano

Peel prawns, leaving tails intact. To butterfly prawns, cut halfway through the back, remove vein, then press flat.
Melt butter in small saucepan; add garlic, capers and oregano. Remove from heat.
Cook prawns on heated, oiled grill plate or barbecue until browned on one side; turn, spoon over some of the butter mixture, cook until just cooked through.
Serve with remaining butter mixture.

serves 4
per serving 17.2g fat; 1091kJ (261 cal)

blue-eye cutlets with pesto butter

60g butter
2 tablespoons basil pesto
$1/4$ teaspoon cracked black pepper
1 teaspoon finely grated lemon rind
4 blue-eye cutlets (1kg)
100g baby spinach leaves, trimmed

Blend or process butter, pesto, pepper and rind in small bowl until well combined.
Cook fish, in batches, on heated oiled grill plate or barbecue until browned and cooked as desired.
Top fish with pesto butter; cook until butter melts. Serve with baby spinach leaves and, if desired, slices of lemon.

serves 4
per serving 24.5g fat; 1584kJ (379 cal)

cajun blue-eye cutlets with lime

2 teaspoons ground cumin
2 teaspoons ground coriander
2 teaspoons sweet paprika
2 teaspoons mustard powder
2 teaspoons onion powder
½ teaspoon garlic powder
¼ teaspoon cayenne pepper
2 teaspoons fennel seeds
4 blue-eye cutlets (1kg)
2 limes, sliced thickly

Combine spices, powders, pepper and seeds with fish in large bowl. Coat fish all over in spice mixture.

Cook fish, in batches, on heated oiled grill plate or barbecue until browned both sides and cooked as desired.

Meanwhile, cook lime on same grill plate or barbecue until browned both sides.

Divide fish among serving plates; top with lime slices.

serves 4
per serving 5.9g fat; 1078kJ (258 cal)
tip Any firm white fish, such as ling, can be used instead of blue-eye. You can use ⅓ cup bottled cajun spice mix, available from supermarkets, instead of making your own, if preferred.

tuna with mixed vegetable stir-fry

*Tuna is best when both sides have been seared and the
centre is fairly rare; overcooking can render this fish dry
and unpalatable.*

1/4 cup (60ml) sweet
  chilli sauce
1/4 cup (60ml) lime juice
1 tablespoon chopped
  fresh coriander
6 tuna steaks (1.2kg)
2 tablespoons finely
  grated lime rind
1 small fresh red
  thai chilli, seeded,
  chopped finely
1 clove garlic, crushed
2 medium zucchini (240g)
2 medium carrots (240g)
2 medium red
  capsicums (400g),
  sliced thinly
1 medium yellow
  capsicum (200g),
  sliced thinly
1 small red onion (100g),
  sliced thinly

Combine sauce, 2 teaspoons of the juice and
coriander in small bowl.

Combine remaining juice in large bowl with tuna,
rind, chilli and garlic. Cover; refrigerate 1 hour.

Meanwhile, cut zucchini and carrots into
very thin slices lengthways; cut slices into
matchstick-sized pieces.

Drain tuna; cook, in batches, on heated oiled
grill plate or barbecue until browned and cooked
as desired.

Meanwhile, heat oiled wok or large non-stick
frying pan; cook 1 tablespoon of the chilli sauce
mixture, zucchini, carrot, capsicums and onion,
in batches, until vegetables are just tender.

Serve tuna on vegetables, drizzled with
remaining chilli sauce mixture.

serves 6
per serving 12g fat; 1517kJ (363 cal)

garfish with sweet cucumber and peanut sauce

¼ cup (55g) caster sugar
½ cup (125ml) water
¼ cup (60ml) lime juice
1 tablespoon fish sauce
2 medium fresh red
  chillies, sliced
1 teaspoon grated
  fresh ginger
18 whole garfish (1.5kg),
  cleaned
cooking-oil spray
1 lebanese cucumber
  (130g), peeled,
  seeded, chopped
1 green onion,
  sliced thinly
1 tablespoon chopped
  fresh coriander
1 tablespoon chopped
  toasted peanuts

To make sauce, combine sugar and the water in small saucepan; cook, stirring, without boiling, until sugar dissolves. Bring to a boil; simmer, uncovered, until reduced by half.

Remove syrup from heat, stir in juice, fish sauce, chilli and ginger; cool.

Meanwhile, spray garfish on each side with cooking-oil spray. Cook garfish, in batches, on heated oiled grill plate or barbecue until browned and cooked through.

Just before serving, stir remaining ingredients into sauce.

Serve garfish with sauce and, if desired, thick char-grilled lime slices.

serves 6
per serving 3g fat; 761kJ (182 cal)
tip The sweet cucumber and peanut sauce can be made four days ahead; store, covered, in the refrigerator.

herbed polenta with tomato salad and chilli mayonnaise

2 cups (500ml) water
2 cups (500ml) vegetable stock
1 cup (170g) polenta
½ cup (40g) finely grated
  parmesan cheese
1 tablespoon chopped fresh
  flat-leaf parsley
1 tablespoon chopped
  fresh basil
1 small fresh red thai chilli,
  seeded, chopped finely

tomato salad
100g mesclun
200g semi-dried tomatoes
4 green onions, sliced thinly
¼ cup (50g) black olives,
  seeded, sliced thinly

chilli mayonnaise
1 cup (300g) mayonnaise
2 small fresh red thai chillies,
  chopped finely
¼ teaspoon ground cumin
¼ teaspoon ground coriander
¼ teaspoon ground turmeric
pinch chilli powder
1 teaspoon sugar
1 tablespoon lemon juice
1 tablespoon chopped
  fresh flat-leaf parsley

Place the water and stock in large saucepan; bring to a boil. Add polenta in a slow, steady stream, stirring constantly. Reduce heat; simmer, uncovered, stirring constantly, about 20 minutes or until polenta thickens. Stir in cheese, herbs and chilli.

Spread polenta mixture into oiled deep 19cm-square cake pan; press firmly to ensure even thickness. When cool, cover; refrigerate about 2 hours or until firm.

Turn polenta onto board; trim edges. Cut polenta into four squares; cut each square in half diagonally. Cook polenta triangles on heated oiled grill plate or barbecue until browned both sides.

Top polenta with tomato salad and chilli mayonnaise.

Tomato salad Gently toss ingredients in medium bowl.

Chilli mayonnaise Combine ingredients in small bowl.

serves 4
per serving 32.8g fat; 2617kJ (626 cal)

glossary

beef

    eye fillet: tenderloin, fillet.

    scotch fillet steak: also known as beef rib-eye steaks.

blue-eye also known as deep sea trevalla or trevally and blue-eye cod; thick, moist white-fleshed fish.

bok choy also known as bak choy, pak choi, chinese white cabbage or chinese chard. Has a fresh, mild mustard taste; use stems and leaves.

butter use salted or unsalted (sweet) butter; 125g is equal to one stick of butter.

capers grey-green buds of a warm-climate shrub, sold either dried and salted or pickled in a vinegar brine; baby capers are tiny, fuller-flavoured and more expensive than full-sized capers. Rinse capers thoroughly before use.

capsicum also known as bell pepper or, simply, pepper. Discard membranes and seeds before use; available in several colours, each of which has an individual flavour.

cayenne pepper thin-fleshed, long, very-hot red chilli; usually purchased dried and ground.

cheese

    fetta: white cheese with milky, fresh acidity; most commonly made from cow milk, though sheep- and goat-milk varieties are available. Matured in brine, which imparts a strong salty flavour. Fetta is solid but crumbles readily.

    parmesan: also known as parmigiano, parmesan is a hard, grainy cow-milk cheese which originated in the Parma region of Italy.

chicken

    breast fillet: breast halved, skinned and boned.

    tenderloins: thin strip of meat lying just under the breast.

    thigh fillet: skin and bone removed from thigh.

chickpeas also called garbanzos, hummus or channa; an irregularly round, sandy-coloured legume used extensively in Mediterranean and Latin cooking.

chilli powder the Asian variety is the hottest, made from dried ground thai chillies; it can be used as a substitute for fresh chillies in proportion of ½ teaspoon chilli powder to 1 medium fresh chilli.

cinnamon dried inner bark of the shoots of cinnamon tree; comes in stick or ground form.

cloves dried flower buds of a tropical tree; can be used whole or in ground form. Have a strong scent and taste so should be used minimally.

cooking-oil spray we used a cholesterol-free cooking spray made from canola oil.

coriander

    ground or seeds: coriander seeds and ground coriander are no substitute for fresh coriander or vice versa.

    fresh: also known as pak chee, cilantro or chinese parsley; bright-green leafy herb with a pungent flavour.

couscous fine, grain-like cereal product, made from semolina.

cumin also known as zeera.

eggplant also known as aubergine.

fennel seeds dried seeds having a licorice flavour.

fish sauce also known as nam pla or nuoc nam. Made from pulverised, salted, fermented fish (most often anchovies); has a pungent smell and strong taste.

five-spice powder a fragrant mixture of ground cinnamon, clove, star anise, sichuan pepper and fennel seeds.

green peppercorns soft, unripe berry of pepper plant, usually sold packed in brine.

hoisin sauce a thick, sweet and spicy Chinese paste made from salted, fermented soy beans, onions and garlic.

hokkien noodles also known as stir-fry noodles; fresh wheat noodles somewhat resembling thick, yellow-brown spaghetti. Need no pre-cooking before being used.

horseradish cream prepared paste of grated horseradish, vinegar, oil and sugar.

lebanese cucumber long, slender and thin-skinned; also known as the european or burpless cucumber.

lamb

    cutlets: small, tender rib chop.

    eye of loin: a cut derived from a row of loin chops. Once the bone and fat are removed, the larger portion is referred to as the eye of the loin.

    forequarter chops: from the shoulder end of the sheep.

lemon grass a tall, clumping, lemon-smelling and -tasting, sharp-edged grass; the white lower part of the stem is used.

lemon pepper also known as lemon pepper seasoning; blend of crushed black pepper, lemon, herbs and spices.

mayonnaise we use whole-egg mayonnaise in our recipes.

mesclun a salad mix of young lettuce and other green leaves.

mushrooms, flat large, flat mushrooms with a rich, earthy flavour.

mustard

powder: finely ground white (yellow) mustard seeds.

wholegrain: also known as seeded. French-style coarse-grain mustard made from crushed mustard seeds and dijon-style french mustard.

oil

olive: made from ripened olives. Extra virgin and virgin are the best; extra light or light refers to taste not fat levels.

peanut: pressed from ground peanuts; most commonly used oil in Asian cooking because of its high smoke point.

sesame: made from roasted, crushed, white sesame seeds; a flavouring rather than a cooking medium.

onion

green: also known as scallion or, incorrectly, shallot; immature onion picked before bulb has formed, having a long, bright-green edible stalk.

powder: dried ground onion. Available from supermarkets.

red: also known as spanish, red spanish or bermuda onion; sweet, large, purple-red onion.

oyster sauce rich sauce made from oysters and their brine, salt, soy sauce and starches.

pancetta cured pork belly; bacon can be substituted.

paprika ground dried red capsicum (bell pepper), available sweet or hot.

pesto a paste made from fresh basil, oil, garlic, pine nuts and parmesan cheese.

polenta cereal made of ground corn (maize); like cornmeal but finer and lighter in colour. Also the name of dish made from it.

pork fillets skinless, boneless eye-fillet cut from the loin.

prawns also known as shrimp.

raisins dried sweet grapes.

rice

basmati: a white, fragrant long-grained rice.

long-grain: elongated grain, stays separate when cooked.

sesame seeds tiny oval seeds available in black and white.

sichuan peppercorns also known as szechuan or chinese pepper. Small, reddish-brown berries with distinctive peppery-lemon flavour and aroma.

snow pea sprouts tender new growths of snow peas.

sour cream thick commercially-cultured soured cream.

spinach also known as english spinach and, incorrectly, silverbeet.

squid is a type of mollusc; also known as calamari.

stock 1 cup (250ml) stock is the equivalent of 1 cup (250ml) water plus 1 stock cube (or 1 teaspoon stock powder).

sugar we used table sugar, also known as crystal sugar, unless otherwise specified.

brown: a soft, fine granulated sugar retaining molasses for its colour and flavour.

caster: also called superfine or finely granulated table sugar.

sweet chilli sauce thai sauce made from red chillies, sugar, garlic and vinegar.

teriyaki marinade a blend of soy sauce, wine, vinegar and spices.

thai chilli bright-red to dark-green in colour; among the hottest of chillies.

tofu also known as bean curd; made from "milk" of crushed soy beans. Comes fresh (soft or firm) and processed (fried or pressed dried sheets).

tomato

cherry: also known as tiny tim or tom thumb tomatoes.

egg: also called plum or roma; smallish and oval-shaped.

semi-dried: partially dried tomatoes in oil.

yellow teardrop: small yellow pear-shaped tomatoes.

turmeric also known as kamin; related to galangal and ginger. Must be grated or pounded to release its pungent flavour.

veal T-bone T-shaped bone with fillet eye attached.

vinegar

balsamic: authentic only from Modena, Italy; made from wine of white Trebbiano grapes.

cider: made from fermented apples.

red wine: based on fermented red wine.

white wine: based on fermented white wine.

wasabi asian horseradish used to make pungent, green sauce served with Japanese raw fish dishes; sold in powder or paste form.

watercress a peppery green; highly perishable.

yogurt we used unflavoured full-fat yogurt in our recipes.

zucchini also known as courgette.

index

conversion chart

MEASURES

One Australian metric measuring cup holds approximately 250ml, one Australian metric tablespoon holds 20ml, one Australian metric teaspoon holds 5ml.

The difference between one country's measuring cups and another's is within a two- or three-teaspoon variance, and will not affect your cooking results. North America, New Zealand and the United Kingdom use a 15ml tablespoon.

All cup and spoon measurements are level. The most accurate way of measuring dry ingredients is to weigh them. When measuring liquids, use a clear glass or plastic jug with the metric markings.

We use large eggs with an average weight of 60g.

DRY MEASURES

METRIC	IMPERIAL
15g	½oz
30g	1oz
60g	2oz
90g	3oz
125g	4oz (¼lb)
155g	5oz
185g	6oz
220g	7oz
250g	8oz (½lb)
280g	9oz
315g	10oz
345g	11oz
375g	12oz (¾lb)
410g	13oz
440g	14oz
470g	15oz
500g	16oz (1lb)
750g	24oz (1½lb)
1kg	32oz (2lb)

LIQUID MEASURES

METRIC	IMPERIAL
30ml	1 fluid oz
60ml	2 fluid oz
100ml	3 fluid oz
125ml	4 fluid oz
150ml	5 fluid oz (¼ pint/1 gill)
190ml	6 fluid oz
250ml	8 fluid oz
300ml	10 fluid oz (½ pint)
500ml	16 fluid oz
600ml	20 fluid oz (1 pint)
1000ml (1 litre)	1¾ pints

LENGTH MEASURES

METRIC	IMPERIAL
3mm	⅛in
6mm	¼in
1cm	½in
2cm	¾in
2.5cm	1in
5cm	2in
6cm	2½in
8cm	3in
10cm	4in
13cm	5in
15cm	6in
18cm	7in
20cm	8in
23cm	9in
25cm	10in
28cm	11in
30cm	12in (1ft)

OVEN TEMPERATURES

These oven temperatures are only a guide for conventional ovens.
For fan-forced ovens, check the manufacturer's manual.

	°C (CELSIUS)	°F (FAHRENHEIT)	GAS MARK
Very slow	120	250	½
Slow	150	275 – 300	1 – 2
Moderately slow	170	325	3
Moderate	180	350 – 375	4 – 5
Moderately hot	200	400	6
Hot	220	425 – 450	7 – 8
Very hot	240	475	9

Are you missing some of the world's favourite cookbooks?

The Australian Women's Weekly cookbooks are available from bookshops, cookshops, supermarkets and other stores all over the world. You can also buy direct from the publisher, using the order form below.

MINI SERIES £2.50 190X138MM 64 PAGES

TITLE	QTY	TITLE	QTY	TITLE	QTY
4 Fast Ingredients		Curries		Pasta	
15-minute Feasts		Drinks		Pickles and Chutneys	
30-minute Meals		Fast Fish		Potatoes	
50 Fast Chicken Fillets		Fast Food for Friends		Risotto	
After-work Stir-fries		Fast Soup		Roast	
Barbecue		Finger Food		Salads	
Barbecue Chicken		From the Shelf		Seafood	
Barbecued Seafood		Gluten-free Cooking		Simple Slices	
Biscuits, Brownies & Biscotti		Ice-creams & Sorbets		Simply Seafood	
Bites		Indian Cooking		Skinny Food	
Bowl Food		Italian		Stir-fries	
Burgers, Rösti & Fritters		Jams & Jellies		Summer Salads	
Cafe Cakes		Kids Party Food		Tapas, Antipasto & Mezze	
Cafe Food		Last-minute Meals		Thai Cooking	
Casseroles		Lebanese Cooking		Thai Favourites	
Char-grills & Barbecues		Malaysian Favourites		Vegetarian	
Cheesecakes, Pavlovas & Trifles		Microwave		Vegetarian Stir-fries	
Chocolate		Mince		Vegie Main Meals	
Chocolate Cakes		Muffins		Wok	
Christmas Cakes & Puddings		Noodles		TOTAL COST	£
Cocktails		Party Food			

Photocopy and complete coupon below

Name _____

Address _____

_____ Postcode _____

Country _____ Phone (business hours) _____

Email*(optional) _____
* By including your email address, you consent to receipt of any email regarding this magazine, and other emails which inform you of ACP's other publications, products, services and events, and to promote third party goods and services you may be interested in.

I enclose my cheque/money order for £ _____

or please charge £ _____ to my:

☐ Bankcard ☐ Mastercard ☐ Visa ☐ American Express ☐ Diners Club

Card number | | | | | | | | | | | | | | | |

Cardholder's signature _____ Expiry date ____ /____

To order: Mail or fax – photocopy or complete the order form above, and send your credit card details or cheque payable to: Australian Consolidated Press (UK), Moulton Park Business Centre, Red House Road, Moulton Park, Northampton NN3 6AQ, phone (+44) (01) 604 497531, fax (+44) (01) 604 497533, e-mail books@acpmedia.co.uk. Or order online at www.acpuk.com
Non-UK residents: We accept the credit cards listed on the coupon, or cheques, drafts or International Money Orders payable in sterling and drawn on a UK bank. Credit card charges are at the exchange rate current at the time of payment.
Postage and packing UK: Add £1.00 per order plus 25p per book.
Postage and packing overseas: Add £2.00 per order plus 50p per book.
Offer ends 30.06.2006